I0427317

101 Poems of Love and Life; Teaching Kids How to Rhyme

by Anadelfa Samson-Bernardo

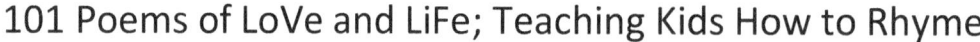

To God be all the glory!

Dedication

To Eg and Kim,

My Nanay, Papa, Peping

First Copyright January, 2024

ISBN 9798876885753

Kindle Direct Publishing, Amazon

National Book Development Board

Table of Contents

Foreword

Curiously, the first part of this rhyme-and-coffee-table book is the produce of several years teaching the English language.

I remember the fun when my students had tried catching for words that they could use while inventing their own rhymes, and when they had completed and the small sheets of paper had been passed in front, they felt victorious. It was an activity that was both hilarious and educational.

However, the limitation of this literature is the metrical footing of a line (in iambic pentameter, it is ten syllables in sonnets and tercets). A number are used as examples although many are written with the end-line rhyming and technique, and that is to achieve the desired playful, enjoyable, and more personalized effect.

This book makes sonnets easier to understand and providing a reference and patterns from which they can launch and create their own verses, lyrical poems or ditties, or even raps which are the more fashionable nowadays; Shakespearean,

Petrarchan or Italian sonnets; limericks, terza-rima stanzas, and haikus, and choose their rhyming patterns. I sincerely hope that elementary, or junior and senior high school students can benefit from these poetic attempts.

The second part is my early poetry. That's when I was counting posts or was pretty bored, and all I did was look at blank walls and try creating sensible written materials. At times, I found myself funny doing so. I hope you will have fun, too, as you try to be creative with words as a tool.

The drawings are sketches of my then eight and ten-year-old sons, some are original; a few may have been copied from books, magazines, or other materials, I honestly do not recall anymore, but it isn't the intention of the writer to violate any copyright laws since I thought that these are pure child sketches and it feels good to have kept and preserved drawings that had been crafted by small hands over the years. You can do your own verses and maybe personalize your own book also.

Finally, have fun reading!

-Author-

Background

Timeless are the works of great masters of art. Shakespeare's sonnets (meaning, fourteen line-poem) for one-- that in one's maturing, an observer said, you will know that they are classic not only because of the beauty of the lines, but because of the truths embed, and with the passing of time, the truths in the lines become more illuminated. Let's take sonnet 50:

1st quartet

How heavy do I journey on the way,
When what I seek, my weary travel's end,
Doth teach that ease and that repose to say,
"Thus far the miles are measur'd from thy friend!"

2nd quartet

The beast that bears me, tired with my woe,
Plods dully on, to bear that weight in me,
As if by some instinct the wretch did know
His rider lov'd not speed, being made from thee:

3rd quartet

The bloody spur cannot provoke him on,
That sometimes anger thrusts into his hide;

Which heavily he answers with a groan, more sharp to
me than spurring to his side;

Concluding lines.

For that same groan doth put this in my mind;
My grief lies onward, and my joy behind.

Shakespearean sonnet is made of three quartets and two concluding lines or the couplets, with a rhyming pattern of ABAB CDCD EFEF GG. The ending rhymes have been color-coded for easy cognition.

Here is an example of Alexander Pope's metrical technique.

1st quartet.

'Tis not enough no harshness gives offense,

The sound must seem an echo to the sense.

Soft is the strain when Zephyr gently blows,

And the smooth stream in smoother numbers flows.

2nd quartet

But when loud surges lash the sounding shore,

The hoarse rough verse should like the torrent roar.

When Ajax strives some rock's vast weight to throw,

The line too labors and the words move slow;

2 Concluding lines.

Not so, when swift Camilla scours the plain,

Flies o'er th' unbending corn, and skims along the
main.

Pope's metrical pattern is AABB, CCDD. EE. There is rhyming couplet (two lines) in the ending.

Francesco Petracco, one of Italy's greatest writers and scholars during the renaissance, makes use of an octave and a sestet, as with other Italian sonneteers. There are two patterns-- ABBA ABBA CD CD CD or ABBA ABBA CDE CDE. At times, there is a *volta* or "turn" at the beginning of the ninth line. Here is one of Petrarch's poems about *Laura*, the love of his life, and for whom many of his sonnets were composed.

O joyous, blossoming, ever-blessed flowers!

'Mid which my pensive queen her footstep sets;

O plain, that hold'st her words for amulets

And keep'st her footsteps in thy leafy bowers!

O trees, with earliest green of springtime hours,
And all spring's pale and tender violets!
O grove, so dark the proud sun only lets
His blithe rays gild the outskirts of thy towers!

O pleasant country-side! O limpid stream,
That mirrorest her sweet face, her eyes so clear,
And of their living light canst catch the beam!
I envy thee her presence pure and dear.

There is no rock so senseless but I deem
It burns with passion that to mine is near.

There are no limits as to the tercets of Dante in his *Divina Commedia* or the Divine Comedy. The epic poem narrative's rhyming pattern is ABA, BCB, CDC, DED, EFE, and so forth. It uses an iambic pentameter as in Shakespeare or Italian sonnets. At times, though, a line may divert from a rhythmic pattern as the example below. There is also what we call "cantos." The canto establishes the theme of certain segments of the entire poem.

Examples of terza-rima lines taken from Inferno

Be joyous, Florence, you are great indeed,
for over sea and land you beat your wings;
through every part of Hell your name extends!

Among the thieves I found five citizens of yours--
    and such, that shame has taken me;
with them, you can ascend to no high honor.

Meanwhile, we shouldn't forget the dactyls and sponde es of the Beowulf and the Homeric ages. We will not lift lines from *Beowulf* or *The Iliad or Oddysey* because the original authors used old English language. Most of the materials available for these bygone eras are either translations or paraphrases. But dactyls are words— one stressed syllable and two unstressed syllables. Spondees are two accented syllables. They may be expressed in a hexameter line, consisting of six feet, the standard measure in old Greek and Latin poetry.

Examples of dactyls.

fla'-ming-o   te'n-der-ly   bre'v-i-ty

Examples of spondees

sonnet   couplet   buffet

I have also included other forms and indicated the patterns.

The blank pages on the other side of every page are for you to fill in with your customized rhymes.

On some occasions, I breached the iambic-pentameter pattern, but retained the number of line-measure and the ending-rhyme pattern.

Limericks have no metering, only line pattern that goes AABBA.

Blessed

Shakespearean Rhyme

A-The birds my muse, the trees, I am smiling,

B-I cooked my breakfast and I had some tea,

A-Stretched my arms, my body, Oh I'm peeing,

B-A bad habit earned, drinking too much tea.

C-Mother told me to buy some vinegar,

D-She got me some coins; went outside to the neighbor,

C-The town is sleeping yet I can't go far,

D-Mother looked at me, 'what do you stare for?'

E-I said it was dark, it was too early,

F-I told her, 'why don't we go back to bed?'

E-It was chilly, my body was shaky,

F-I went on walking in the dark I tread.

G-' came back with the vinegar, am rhyming,

G-Mother was cooking, I got my timing.

One Beautiful Morning

Petrarchan Rhyme

Octave

A-Fill up my pages with lines endearing,

B-I can have my *pandesal*, make some c'ffee,

B-May I be loving and my whole being,

A-To child and old, to beasts and foes.

A-Inspire me, with good thoughts I am beaming,

B-Kitties went running, I thought they were sleepy.

B-A child has been meandering, wondering.

A-An old book she read, she had missed her key.

Sestet

C-Although she'd missed the key, she sings and runs.

D-The book stories sets her heart a booming.

C-Plants, flowers, shrubs and trees sway and dance,

D-Along with the birds cooing and humming.

C-One beautiful morning I fixed my pants,

D-As I set my feet to walk in the morning.

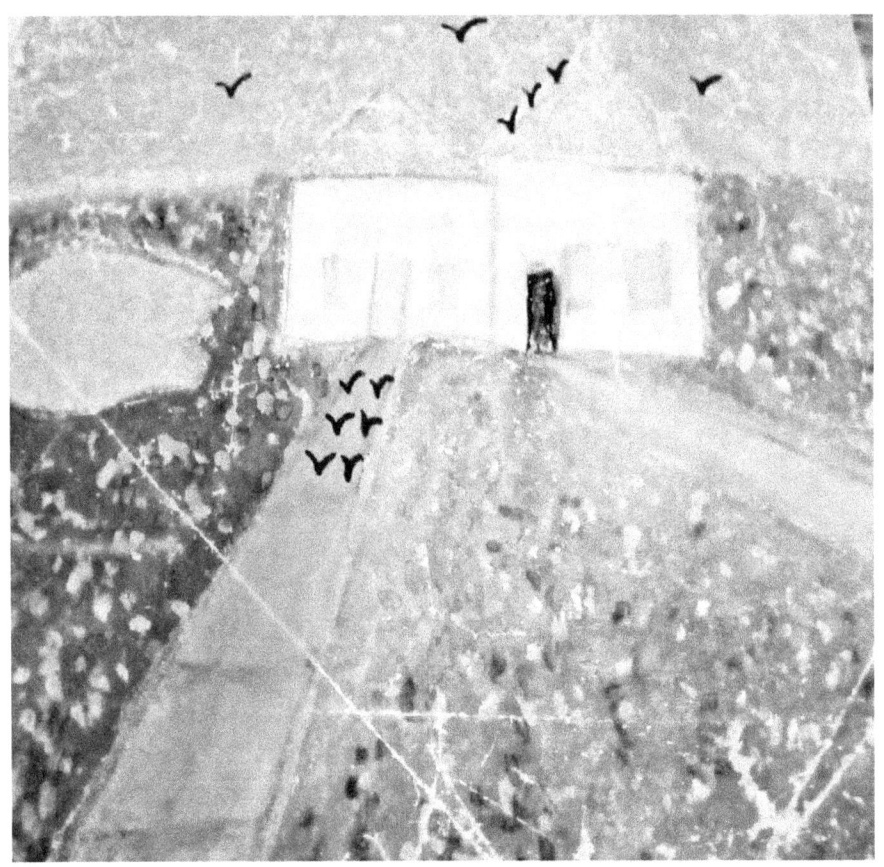

Birds

A-Birds chirp,

B-People chatter,

B-Toys scatter,

A-Nails clipped.

Octave

A-I peeked,

B-Looked at the gutter,

B-Cats clutter!

A-Oh! am at the tip!

C-Got a powder

D-Splashed on my cheek,

C-A make-over

D-Did my beauty keep.

Sestet

C-A little loud, my make-over

D-Laughed as I shrieked.

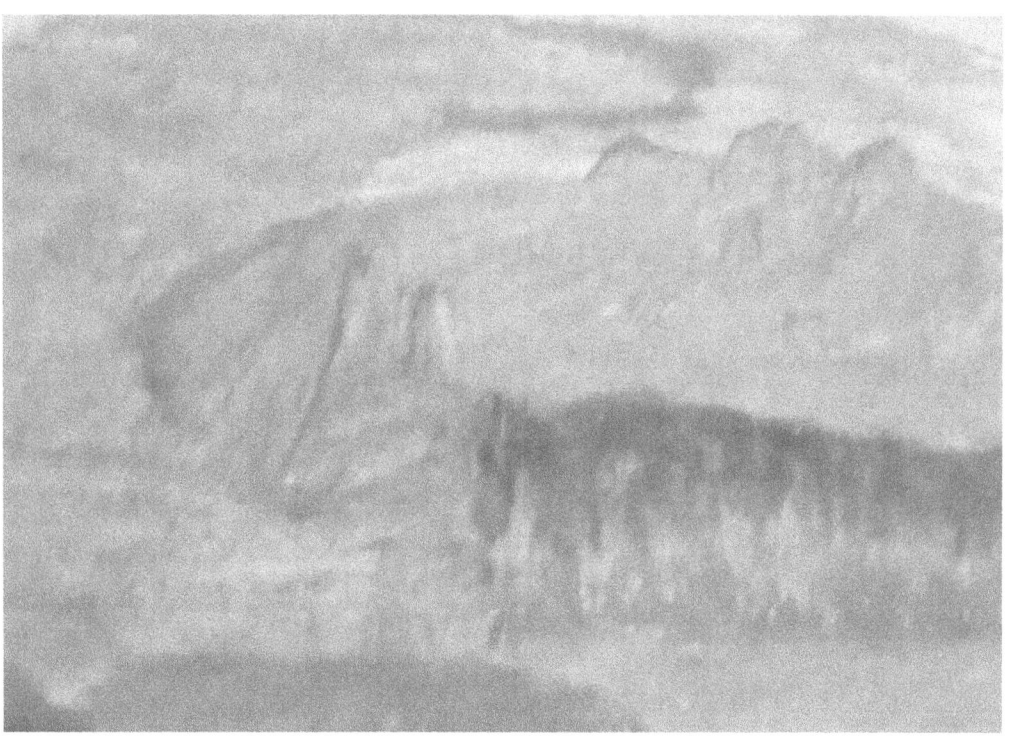

Perseverance

Alexander Pope's Rhyme Pattern

A-The softness of the gentle tweeting birds,

A-The quietness of the strides of herds,

B-You have walked inside without any noise,

B-Then tinker with the usual thing of choice.

C-I was on my laptop building words,

C-Will it have an impact to readers hordes?

D-You went along with your work, you're patient,

D-Whatever resource you're content, you're sentient,

E-There'll always be a new way, you don't complain,

E-Everyday is a new day, nothing is in vain.

Dawn

(Limerick)

A-At the break of dawn,

A-at the break of dawn,

B-I got out of bed,

B-kneeled and said,

A-Thank you God, kids are fully-grown.

God is everywhere

(Free Verse)

God is a god of peace,

in the flowers He created,

in the plants that creep,

and trees that climb

and greet the sky,

in the bushes, thorny

and smooth,

in the cats that meow,

and dogs that bark too,

in beautiful kids, and men

and women,

in the briskly morning,

and in the sun that's high up,

in the lazy moon,

and in breeze that is gentle,

in sun shines,

and in sunsets.

Giggle and Tickle

Limerick

Example 1.

A-Make me giggle.

A-Give me a tickle.

B-Create me a humming.

B-Make me a booming.

A-Shake me up!

Example 2.

A-She tweets, she chirrups;

A-fills my half-empty cup.

B-Coffee is waiting,

B-morning juice 'am making,

A-'am waking up!

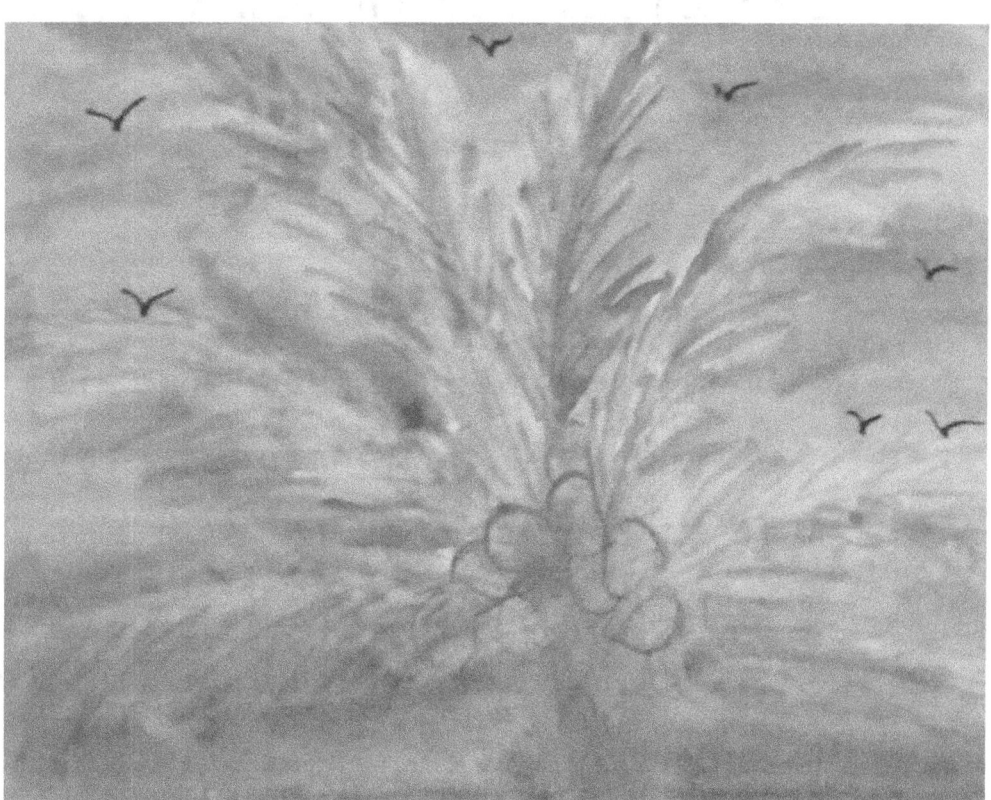

Only God can make a bird sing

Shakespearean Rhyme

A-Only God can make a bird sing,

B-As soft and sweet, and cool,

A-' am by my room but they won't stop humming,

B-Get up they say or we shall give you a pull.

C-We are adventuring, enjoy the day.

D-We're reading a book, don't be a kill joy.

C-A book we ride on, no matter what you say;

D-Yes, a magical book, dig it? Oh boy!

E- She's one of the characters, shake it up!

F- The witch that got the magic ring, beat it!

E- He's the prince that saved the queen, dance it up!

F- He killed the monster in disguise, nail it!

G- Now you are free, do what you want to do,

G- Now you are pretty, do what you have to do.

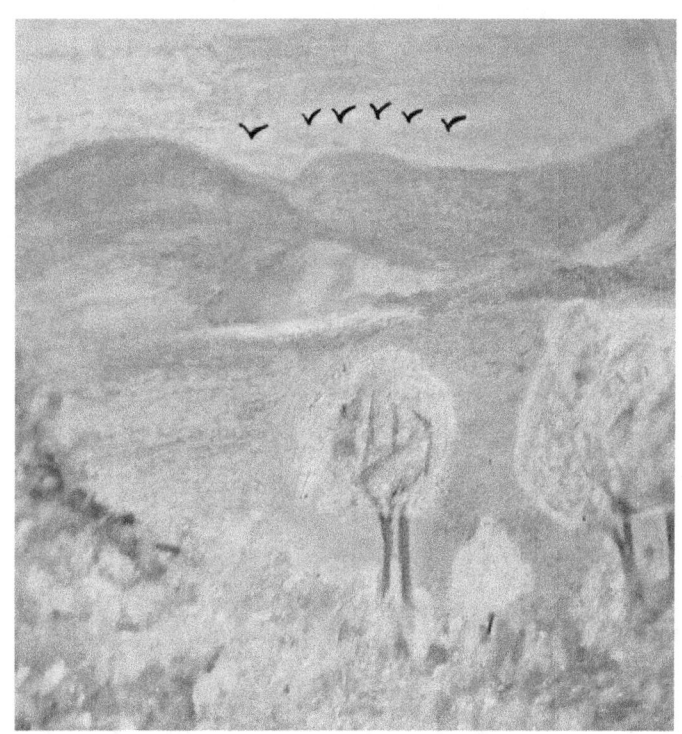

Geeky Bird

Limerick

A-You always try to get my attention,

A-as I am watching the television.

B-Are you jealous of Sherlock Holmes?

B-Or are you a geek who keeps tomes?

A-You're welcome songbirds; you are my love

potion.

Cool Sunrise
Shakespearean Rhyme

A-All is set for good, my body in motion,

B-My brain is right, so won't you get me straight,

A-A pen in my hand, I need an inspiration,

B-I can go to the kitchen, make me bake.

C-Am looking at the fields, Oh! the rustic scene,

D-Yellow, green, and gold colors, how I love!

C-Marinated chickens in the oven, seared,

D-A smell of burnt grass under the sky above.

E-I have cleaned the house with a broom, everything clear,

F-The sun has lit up in the east, everything shin,

E-Watered window pots and plants, the flowers brim,

F-I was done by six a.m., yards are clean.

G-I sat to rest awhile, smells are great!

G-The kitties have started menacing, open up the gate!

Spring

Italian Sonnet

A-Have you been drowned? I don't hear you tweet,

B-Is the rain gone? I haven't heard you chirped,

B-One stumbled on the ground, bouncing like a creep,

A-Another one frowned, shown its tail and teeth.

A-Lost my purse once, life may not be all sweet,

B-You playing around, ' know ' am ahead of the trip,

B-Running here and there, saw a hole and peeped,

A-You brought cheers to my lips, antics ' been a hit.

C-When I could see you dance, I could hear you sing,

D-Step one two three four, 'am running but for sure

C-'am almost at the finish line, I could give you a ring,

D-Give me luck, ideas, I could feel my chance,

C-Don't fret and don't you frown, for the time has come,

D-There's gonna be a romance; it'll always be spring.

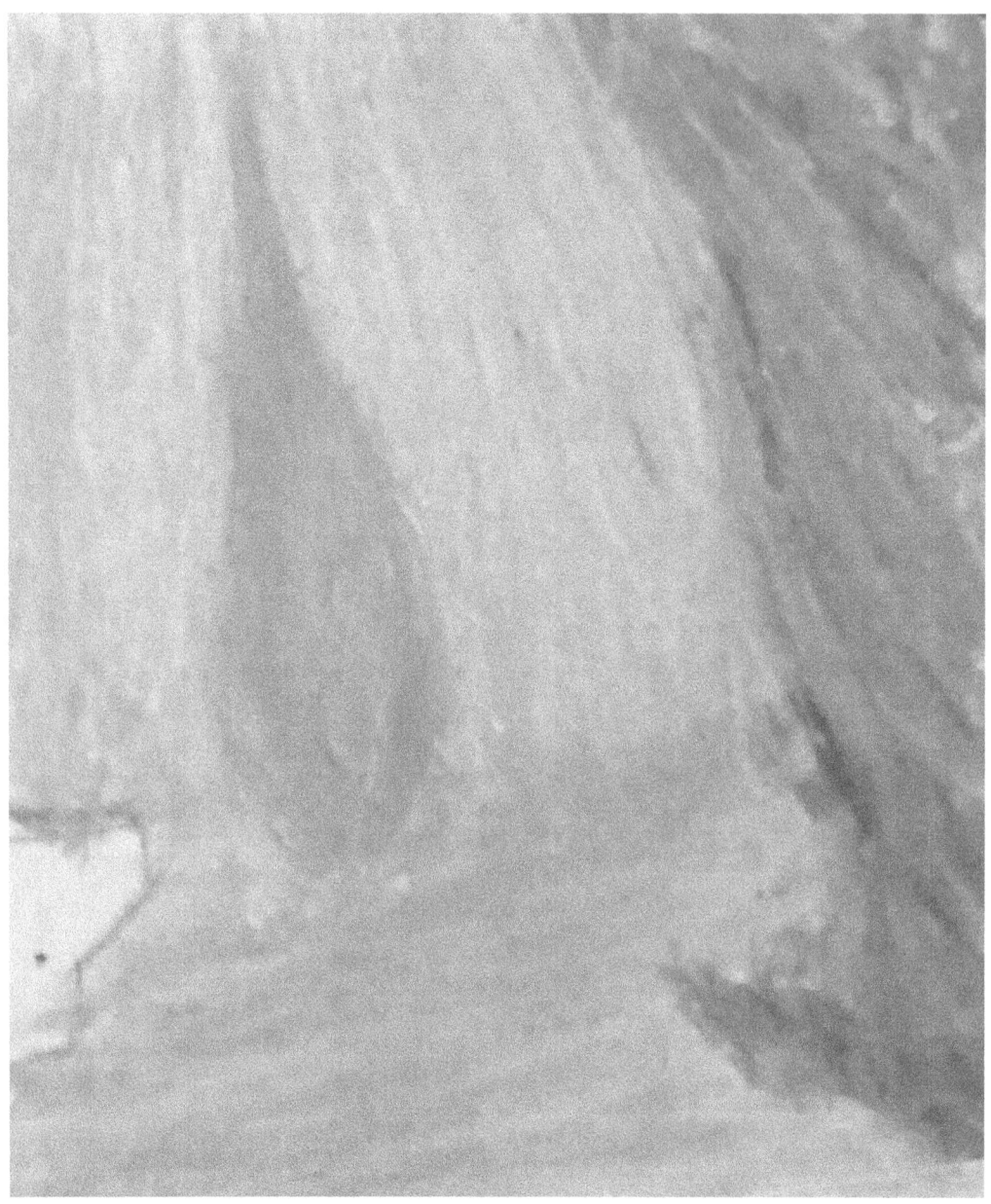

Popping Up

Free Verse

My little birds pop up from

nowhere,

cooing and humming,

laughing and tweeting,

kissing and swinging,

dancing and chattering.

Their joyous merry-making

are so amazing.

Endless they come,

peeping, they gather.

Bloom

Free Verse

Have you ever looked closely at a rose?

Have you seen it changed into many different colors?

Seen it open up its petals upon bloom?

… at its most joyous form and state?

When it sheds its flower, it sheds slowly,

It doesn't cry out;

It sheds quietly,

Have you seen it at its wilting stage?

… noticed that it's even more excitingly gorgeous

    than when you've last seen it?

The changes in its colors,

The form,

The state,

The petals,

The flower,

The subtle wrinkles,

Why doesn't a rose shrink right away when it's about to wilt?

How come it blooms like forever?

Examples of Terza-Rima Stanzas

Example 1.

A-Dunno why ' am thrilled when you chirp close to my ear,

B-I beam, I dream, my zest for life redeemed,

A-You settled on a tree and I sat here, carefree.

Example 2.

A-That's wonderful tweeting, are you talking?

B-Get me to my dreaming, life must be good,

A-Your body is round now, what are you saying?

C-Like the clouds above, looked white, green, fluffy,

D-strong and healthy, blessed no less by God,

C-Like little toddlers, too, in our community.

Example 3.

A-Late in the morning, 'jogged 'round neighborhood,

B-On the way I met a friend, we exchanged hellos,

A-Weather's too hot under the sun clothes baked.

C-Went in the kitchen to heat some water,

D-Fried rice, boiled eggs, steamed a little vegetable,

C-As I was ready, 'prepared the breakfast after.

Example 4.

A-Haven't seen you for a while, are you gone now?

B-I was busy for my teaching lessons,

A-Need my visor, did you pass by, down the aisle? Bow.

Limerick

A-I'm running out of vocabulary,

A-that strays from the ordinary,

B-need to stretch my imagination,

B-so I won't be clinging to my cushion,

A-or I sleep, I'll be dreaming honey.

Y and O/U Rhyming Pattern

I can't be forever clingy,

to one who is stingy,

need to have life, too,

I have to be true,

I got my priorities, can't live in a dingy.

To the Light!

Shakespearean Rhyme

A-Go forth and shine, and to the light go bright.

B-Go forth from darkness we were taken out.

A-Shine bright child, shine bright child with all your might.

B-Run the mile, in your heart, give a loud shout!

C-Heaven's manifest, earth's beauty come 'bout,

D-with you and me as the best precious gems,

C-and gold and silver there is no single doubt,

D-booming and blooming flowers at the hem.

E-Whoo! I shall be dancing to the earth's tune,

F-Yeah!, there's simply nothing that can stop me,

E-because my mind is up to the moon, rune,

F-see, my rhymes are bending naturally.

G-Fly, oh! high. My kite will go up the sky.

G-The larks sing as my kite go up the sky.

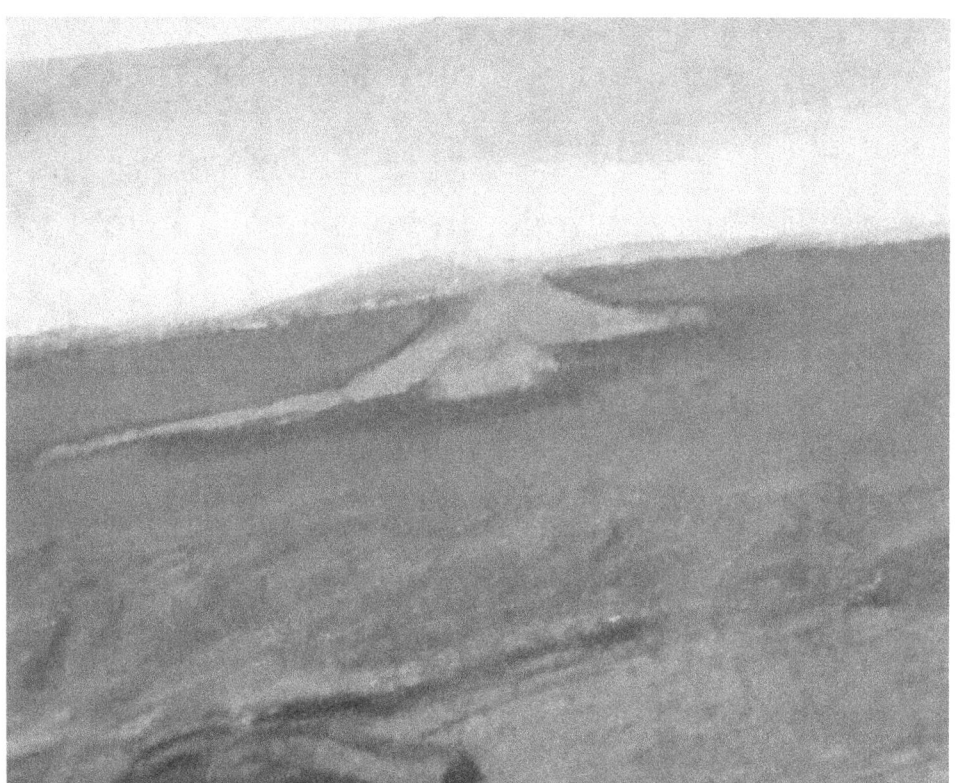

Ing-ending Rhyme Verse

(No pattern)

Merry Christmas!

Thank you for the chirping,

It gave my heart a-thumping,

and my body a jumping,

A peek at my heart,

will show you that it's smiling.

LIMERICK

AABBA

A-Wake up!

A-I got to catch up,

B-My store is waiting,

B-I need to be working,

A-Make some pennies for a living.

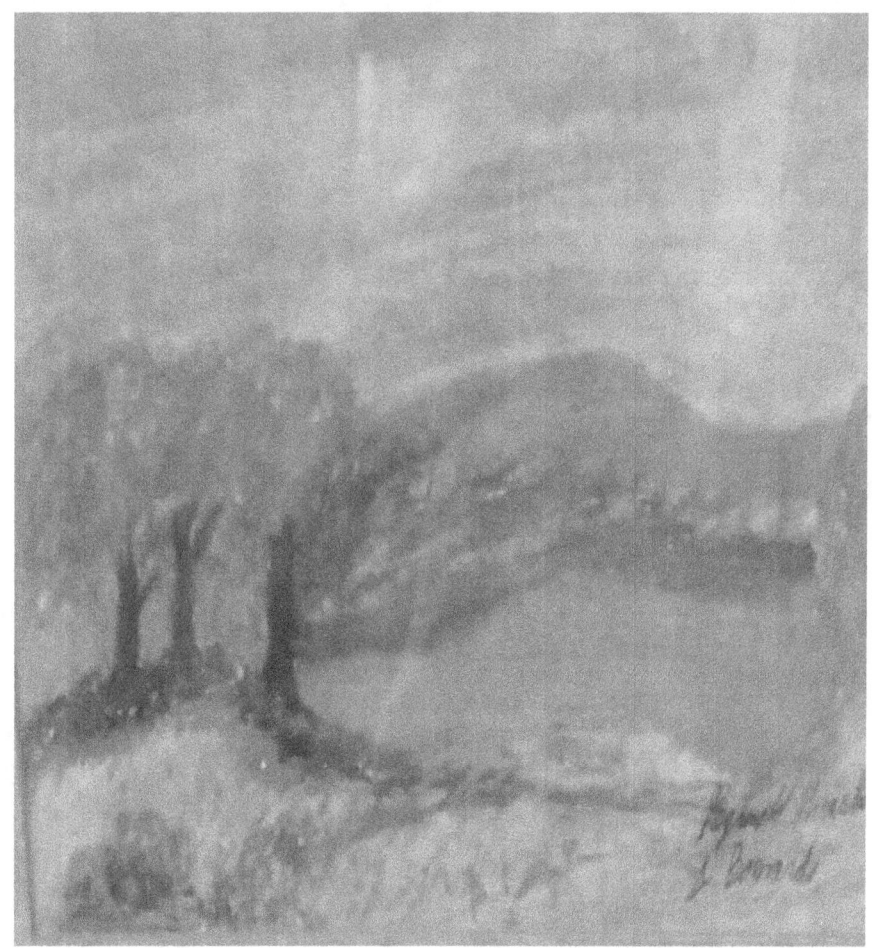

LIMERICK

AABBA

A-Wake up!

A-Get it all up,

B-We'll go for a walking,

B-The day is waiting,

A-Like stars-- for us to be shining.

Rap

(No pattern)

It's a glorious morning!

We can praise God

with your joyous tweeting.

No one can equal

your song.

Oh! funny bird,

You keep calling me, rap.

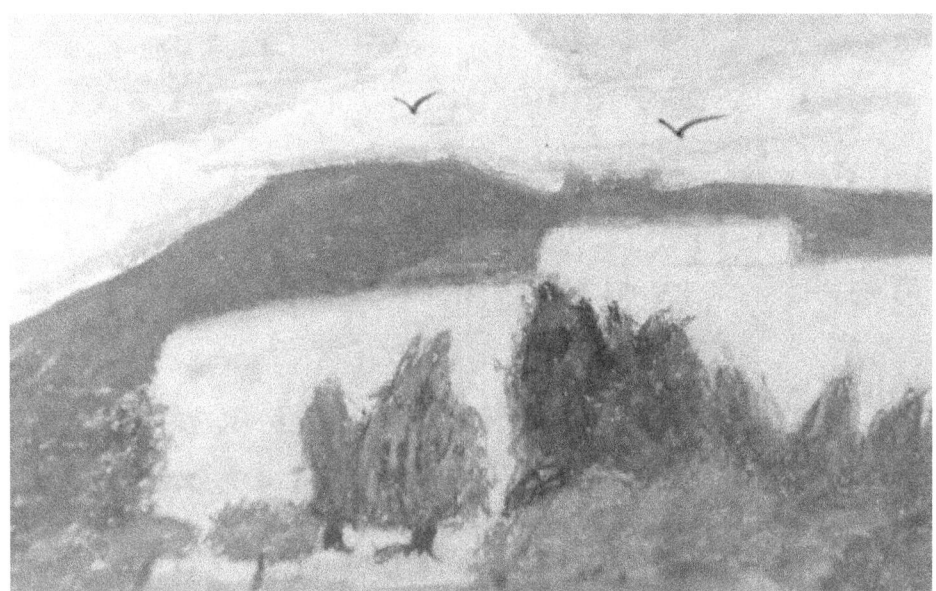

Limerick

AABBA

A-You sing like no one

A-with your melodious hum,

B-Sweeter than a flute, a violin, or any string,

B-How such wonder you sing? Such sweetness you bring,

A-All worries and heartaches are gone.

Limerick

AABBA

A-Have you LOL?

A-Did you bury yourself in the soil?

B-I've missed my toy.

B-Happy New Year, Oh boy!

A-Give me a cake and a foil.

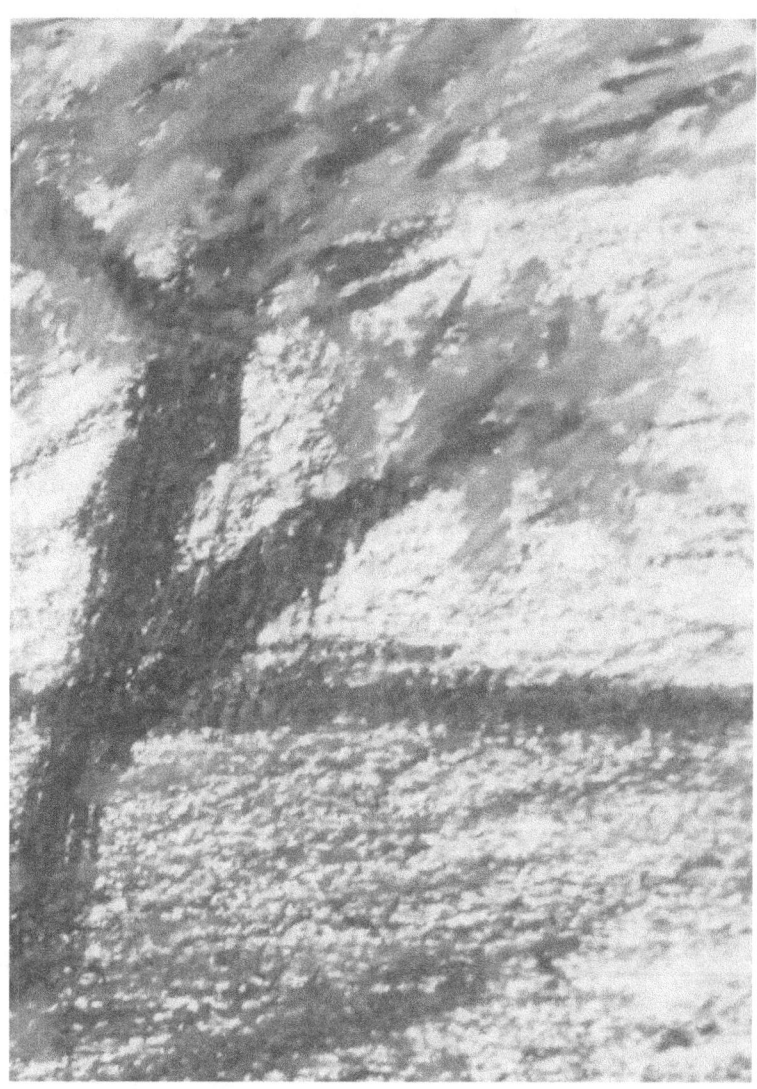

Christmas season is in!

Shakespearean Rhyme

A-You amaze me like flow'rs under the sun,

B-Rock, rock the baby, will you rock it out,

A-Certainly has graced me, ' soul smiles, it's fun,

B-Dance, dance the baby, dance, dance, dance it out!

C-You must be an angel, an angel dear,

D-I'll sing shing-a-ling, shing-a-ling-ding-dong,

C-As you flap your wings, I won't make a sneer,

D-*Bungbong, bibingka* are in, church bells peal, dong!

E-Guide me in the shadows, Lord, be my light,

F-Cheer up, for in simplicity, I thrive,

E-To the light, I shine now, forever bright,

F-Bliss I accomplish, will you be my guide?

G-Fly with me sparrows, dunnocks, small passerine,

G-Fly, Oh! high, sparrows, dunnocks, small passerine.

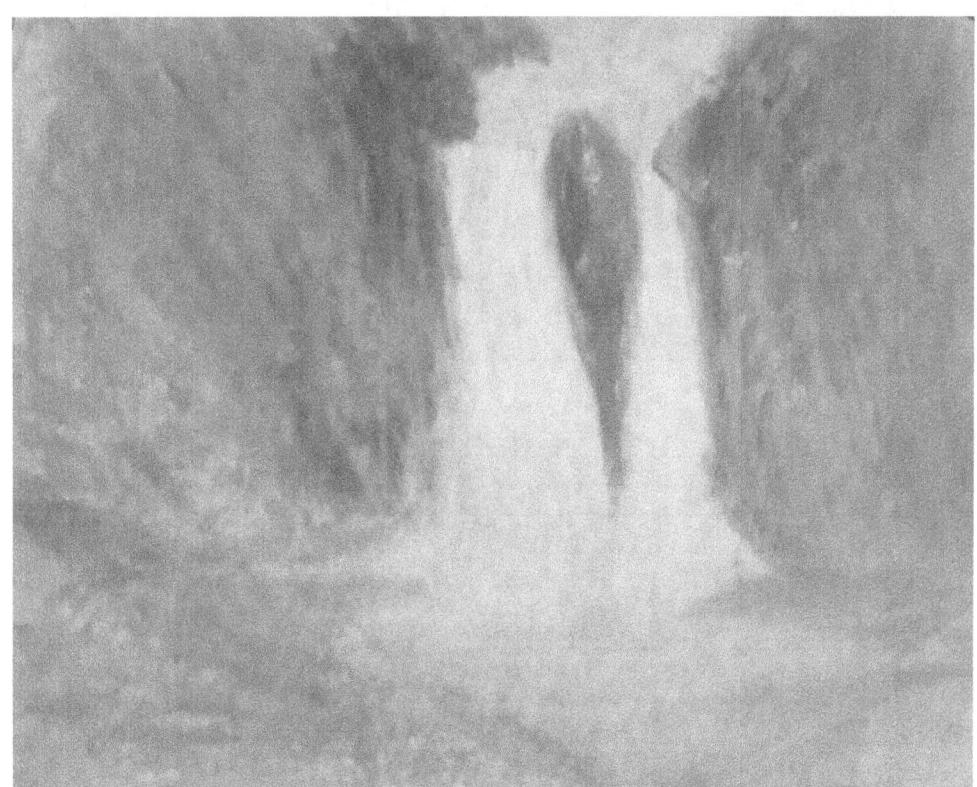

Rhyme Verse

(No pattern)

Bobbing and popping,

'am enthralled.

tell me more,

'wish to do a thing

that will bring this to the core,

I got to live a life,

that is not a bore.

Ordinary Rhyming Pattern

Did you just call me?

You tweeted strongly,

as only a God can be.

You're fantastic,

It isn't much ado,

to listen to your call,

and say I do.

Do that again, tweet a million;

we shall play a peek-a-boo.

Little Creatures of God

Shakespearean Rhyme

A-Little creatures of God that isn't so bad,

B-Flying in flocks, I heard you joyfully sing,

A-I wasn't feeling well, felt terribly bad,

B-but you flew in front of me, ' gave me a zing!

C-How's it that you whisper so gloriously?

D-Your wings must be very light like airplanes,

C-You softly, sweetly whisper copiously,

D-' set up my mood right, there are no more pains.

E-You know I can rise above my station,

F-Writing is a passion like J.K. Rowling,

E-and everything becomes good intention;

F-use imagination, keep my life going.

G-How can you do your job so faithfully?

G-How can you do everything graciously?

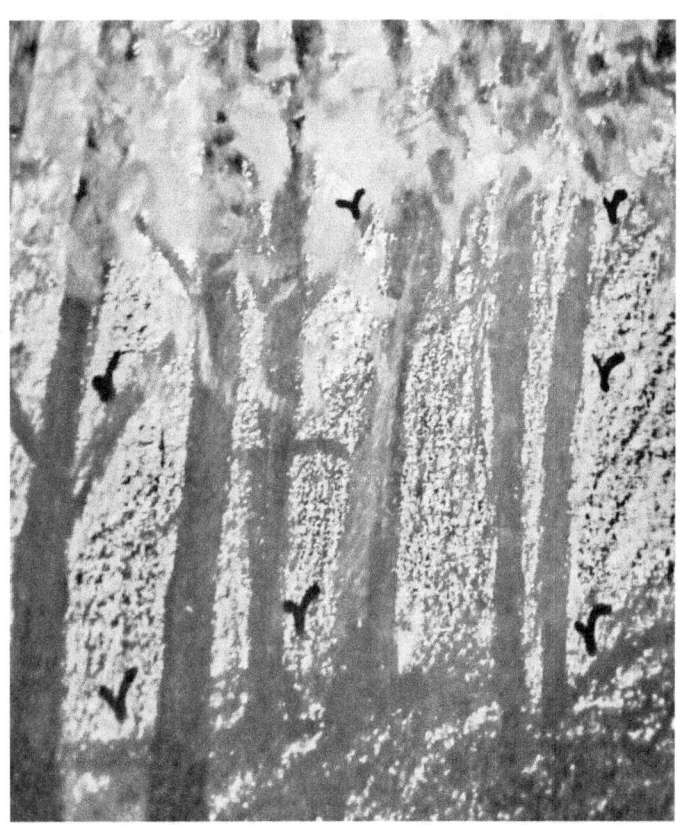

Terza Rima Stanza

A-Where are you. ' haven't heard you for a while,

B-' was too busy for whatchamacallit,

A-Wait up, my friends, I am missing my file.

Pets and Sparrows

Italian Rhyme

A-I miss the humming, I got up early

B-I am looking for what's a faint cooing

B- ' am used to the noise my kitties are making

A-They can be messy, one of them is big-y.

A-They told me they're peeing, ' sent them out quickly,

B-No matter bum-my, they always got me smiling.

B-Among the pots, the four of them went hiding,

A-And among the flowers, ' hide their body.

C-Funny little creatures, you got me droopy.

D-Then from the roof something landed on the ground.

E-The birds sang their songs with full vocal chord.

C-The kittens in return, showed up surprisingly.

D-' did their queenly walk as they were bound -to market to buy fish in their skating board.

Bard

Petrarchan Rhyme

A-Day breaks with a beautiful sunrise.

B-An explosion of morning birds' sweet tweeting

B-to surroundings bring melodious humming.

A-Flowers are in bloom, sunrise bursts and cries.

A- Wake up with an aroma of bacon fries.

B-You're a winner with your gentle endless chirruping

B-Sets her mood as she gets to write in the morning

A-In the oven also are baked pizza pies.

C-Mom had looked for his boy,

D-He's been missing, he was nowhere in the yard,

E-Where had he gone on an early morning?

C-On the floor, she was picking his toys,

D-She heard somebody play like a bard.

E-She had a smile on her lips, his music beckoned.

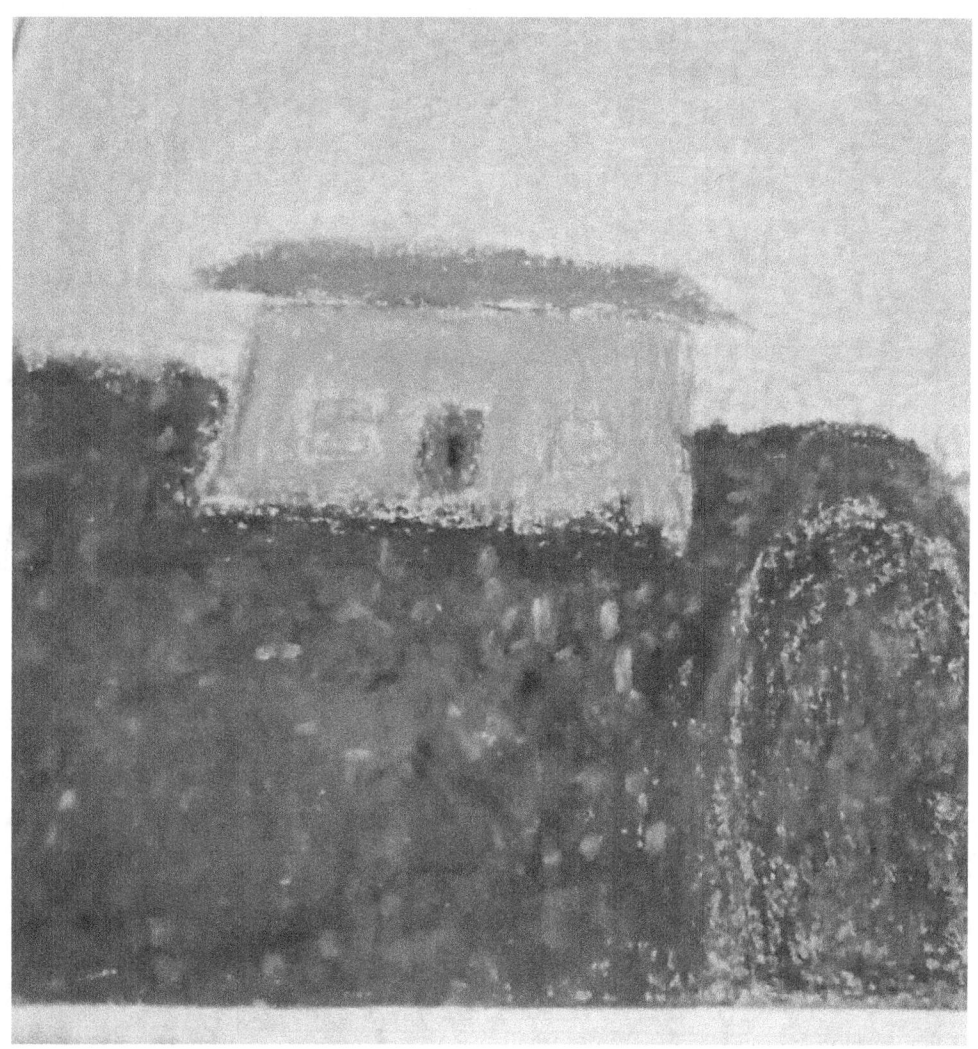

Little Boy

Italian Rhyme

A-You are nowhere, but the TV is on,

B-Come my little gadget, give me a song,

B-I am frying and reaching for the tong.

A-The clothes hanging are waiting to be donned.

A-The birds are gone, rainy season is on,

B-Twas hot a while ago, the game is on,

B-The rain poured down, what d'ya think have you done?

A-Will you give me a break, please turn me on.

C-My boy behaves like a real cowboy,

D-On the floor are scattered all of his toys

E-' made a mess of his room, his car. bumpy.

C-He took the kitty, he really can be a tragedy,

D-' took out of the neighborhood other boys,

E-Stretches the frail arms 'til the cat is limpy.

Fantastic Birds

Italian Rhyme

A-Where are you? Are you hiding in your nest?

B-Haven't seen you for a while, you alright?

B-No cooing, no humming, my angels bright,

A-She flew down with a raincoat, 'miss my

friend best.

A-Come right here, funny birds, you give me rest,

B-You've funny footsteps in the wind and rain,

B-Without your cooing and humming ' am drained,

A-She came sliding down like riding on a crest.

C-You tweet at my back, you're my angel of light,

D-You're fantastic, make everything, to me, brim,

E-Come and dance, come and dance around me.

C-You cooed in front of me, a sweet delight,

D-Called my name as I sleep you're in my dream,

E-Danced a few steps, 'am stronger in my knee.

Ordinary Rhyming Pattern

Example 1.

My mind keeps a churning,

little verses I've been squeezing,

Tweet more, get me a dreaming.

Example 2.

As 'am excited

at the break of day,

Light has shown

in the east, our way,

Give us hope

to the Lord we pray,

Make us whole

to conquer the day.

Feast

Shakespearean Rhyme

A-Now he is singing,

B-Boom, boom, boom,

A-And to the tune he is swinging,

B-A dum, dum, dum.

C-Happily he got to his cooing,

D-Shaking up his booty,

C-Babbling and dancing,

D-Other birds came to his tootling.

E-The little bird came back,

F-Any playmates he didn't have, he frowned,

E-His face was sad, suddenly, "pak!"

F-A worm he saw his body became round.

G-I'll feast on you,

G-but first, I will have to roast you.

Thief

Shakespearean Rhyme

A-They said I'm lazy.

B-They got my mood so I brood.

A-Feel like crazy.

B-'got to invent my livelihood.

C-'needed money.

D-An idea is shaping up, a business I came

up.

C-Down the alley,

D-sold everything I can I've shaped up.

E-Then a thief came, my efforts he disdain.

F-Nothing I can do...

E-My efforts were insane,

F-Nothing I can do.

G-Nothing I gained but sweat and tears,

G-Everything in shame,,, sweat and tears.

Season Of Love

Shakespearean Rhyme

A-Christmas anew is in the air,

B-A gentle ambience is everywhere,

A-Foods, gifts, chocolates, and my hair,

B-Delicious, sumptuous, expensive, pricey... err.

C-The month of spending,

D-One of these days we're gallivanting,

C-Our ego and pride we are bending,

D-Need all these once-a-year break, we shouldn't

be missing.

E-In the mood

F-for some Christmas carols.

G-But I am old

G-I was told, nonetheless, I have become cool.

You got me up!

(A poem with no specific rhyming pattern)

You cooed,

I woke up,

Another coo,

You got me up.

' am on my feet now,

' ready for the walking,

The sky is crying,

Make haste, it might be raining.

Workers On The Planking

(Limericks)

A-Workers are hurrying,

A-Faster they got on the planking,

B-On the pedestrian lane,

B-The cars stopped running, speeding in disdain,

A-People crossed to the next street, they're walking.

A-Ringgg!

A-The bell sounded another "Ringgg!"

B-Faster they walked,

B-Can't be late, as they talked,

A-They have to get moving.

More Limericks

Example 1.

A-Have you been dreaming?

A-Is that the reason why you're smiling?

B-Keep hanging on,

B-It isn't time, work, don't be so much on the phone,

A-Keep moving forward, you'll be rising.

Example 2.

A-Keep moving forward you're not a dead wood,

A-A whole bag of tricks will later turn out good,

B-Don't let grass grow under your feet,

B-Or you will not reach the peak, then, that won't be a feat,

A-Keep moving forward; in the past, don't brood.

Example 3.

A-Slowly, rise up to the challenge,

A-Pretend, that nothing's ever hinged,

B-Because nothing's ever hinged, 'less there's a ghoul,

B-Nothing's ever locked to you, get a tool,

A-Nothing's ever changed?

Let's try the Haiku!

The HAIKU is a poem that originated in Japan. It has a 5-7-5 syllabication for every line, but has no definite rhyming pattern.

Example 1.

Your ditties are like

a very good pizza pie

nothing can equal.

Example 2.

I got to catch you,

You coo, you hum, sing, and run,

You tweet, my posies.

129

Example 3.

A white bird I saw,

Prattles non-sense as she flew,

Flew, she bumps the wall.

Example 4.

Why run, little bird,

Without looking at the road,

Are you terrified?

Example 5.

Oh, funny bird, look,

Did you do a naughty thing?

Fly and flap your wings..

Example 6.

Day is grey, but I'm on my way,

Will you make my mood upbeat

'though my heart is in pain?

Example 7.

How come you can sing,

dance though there ain't things to gain?

Make the day happy.

Example 8.

Heads bobbed up,

up and down, up and down,

Nowhere could we go around.

She runs here and there,

Tailing mommy walked to the rain,

Around this house we can play hide-and-seek.

Then birds popped up from nowhere.

Kitties said we're not too strong yet to jump;

When we're grown up we will run after you.

Example 9.

A-Birds replied.

B-When you've grown up we're old,

A-Weaker, maybe, but wiser.

C-Catch us up you may,

D-We won't get away,

C-But don't pull our tail.

C-And you won't get away,

D-That's for sure,

C-Your conscience catches you up, nay.

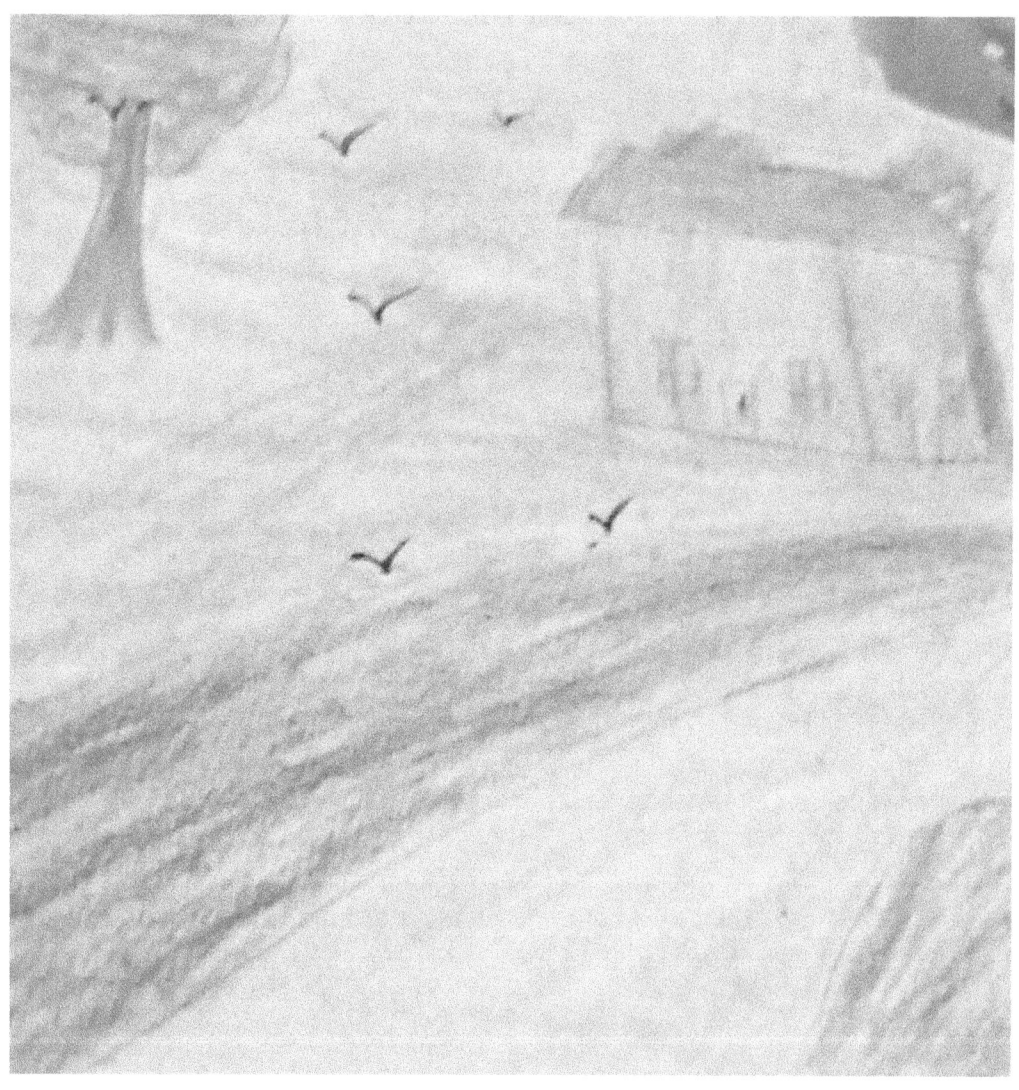

More Limericks

Example 1.

A-Not in my vein to fight,

A-Shed me a light.

B-Need the truth,

B-Get me to my mood,

A-Won't make a blight.

Example 2.

A-To bring food on the table,

A-My job I do I keep I am able,

B-My sheer delight,

B-The future's bright,

A-I had believed I'm capable.

Example 3.

A-Cold wind touching my skin,

A-A relief as I spin,

B-My friend's wit is dying,

B-He was a bit crying,

A-Lost his doll he wasn't keen.

Example 4.

A-Birds are bursting

A-with tweeting and dancing,

B-A map she dropped,

B-Without direction she's trapped,

A-No matter, she kept trudging.

Example 5.

A-Keep moving,

A-Keep fighting,

B-No matter is the taking,

B-No matter is the shaking,

A-Keep dancing.

Example 6.

A-Chances are we grow,

A-We may have lost our way,

B-We sail out,

B-Or bail out,

A-A complex life anyway that's borrowed.

Sunrise

(Free Verse)

Example 1.

Sunrise is up,

but I am still waiting.

My body's all up,

bracing for your blessing.

A smile, a bone, a muscle,

a fool, a dancing,

People, kids, music,

films, prayers,

are all for merry-making.

Example 2.

Endless cooing,

and endless blooming,

of flowers be,

His love amazing,

I am forever gazing

at beauty, oh!

Everywhere it's oozing.

Missing Sock

(Ing-ending Rhyming Pattern)

My funny friend,

I need to be tracing

my pink sock is missing.

While I was sleeping,

can't find this morning.

No matter was I looking

on my bed and under,

and all surroundings,

I am wondering,

if my Lord's talking.

Flying

(No specific rhyming pattern)

Sure, I am glad to have seen you,

Days were dry I had sorely missed you,

How I wish I can fly like you,

and spread my wings, whoo!

to the ends of the earth,

from since they've given me birth,

In my dreams and imagination,

Maybe, I do,

If you'll keep me company, too,

That way have I conquered myself?

That's a big question mark, too.

155

Cooing

(Ion-ending Rhyming Pattern)

One coos to get my attention,

Three sitting on the cushion,

More fly in one direction,

I am amazed at your protection.

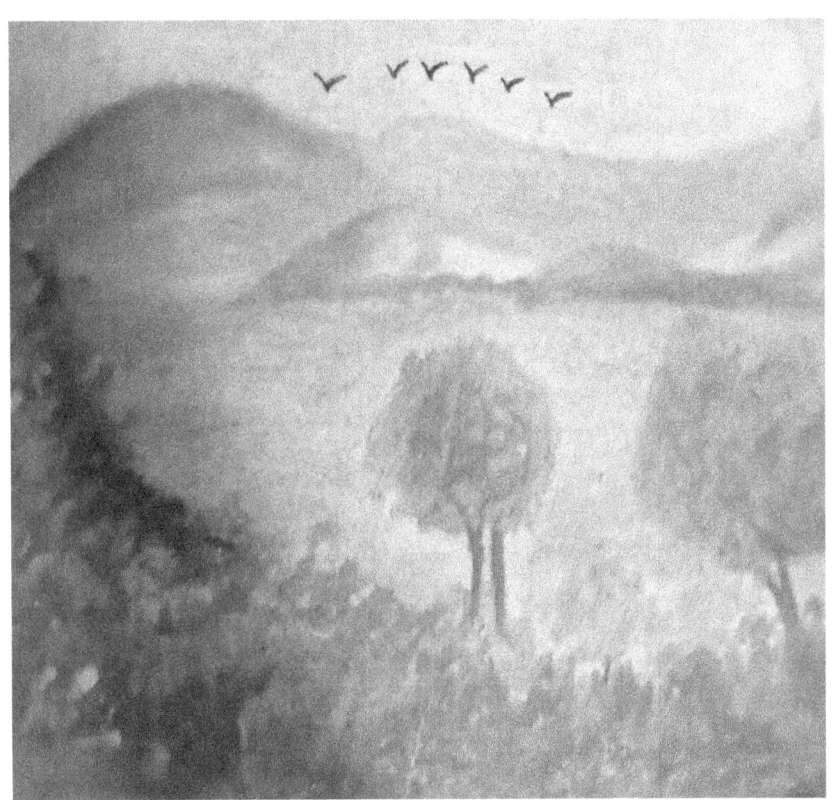

Development

(Free Verse)

I can't hear

the tweeting birds this morning,

The noise is much,

the hums are fainting,

Why can't people see

that they're enough for beauty?

And the flora and fauna

are all they need completely?

Development is in people.

.

Goofy

(Limerick)

A-Lucky, sunny,

A-Happy, groovy,

B-She rode on the cycle,

B-Didn't know it was going to be a bumpy ride,

A-Goofy was the baby.

Rainy days

(A poem with no specific rhyming pattern)

Rainy days,

Wet hays,

Feet cramping,

Ambling on but solid ground.

Look at our ways,

Rubbish haste,

Legs jumping,

Much as it tried it's bound.

Stir up my mood,

Need my coffee brewed.

Light In The Dark
(Free Verse)

You are the Light in the dark,
the smile on my lips,
the snowflakes of winter,
the sun's rays of summer,
the cool breeze and embrace of a windy weather,

You're the happy face I put on,
the reason why I keep dancing,
singing, and weaving my prose and phrases,
You are closest to joy, the inspiration of my heart,
my existential cause,

And when I'm lonely...

You are the spark in the middle
of the night,
the quiet joy against a background
of uncertainties,
my hope beyond distress
and desperation,
sturdiest among breaking vines,
steadiest among drooping
and dying plants,
the very light footsteps
against space and time.

Tickle me

(Free Verse)

Come, help me more,

I need lines tickle me more,

You're like water;

Your droplets of humming

is life.

You're like the plants and trees

that causes the breeze

to whine,

and the sun to shine.

Thank you for the tweeting

(Free Verse)

You've called for me again,

Is it going to be you and me then?

In this world and in my dream,

You are there within my sphere,

Thank you for the tweeting,

I am at my peak

(A poem with no specific rhyming pattern)

There's no stopping,

your wonderful chirruping,

' am up and at my best,

' gonna beat the heat,

' dropped my clicker,

' instead do a leaf-peeping

of this beautiful morning.

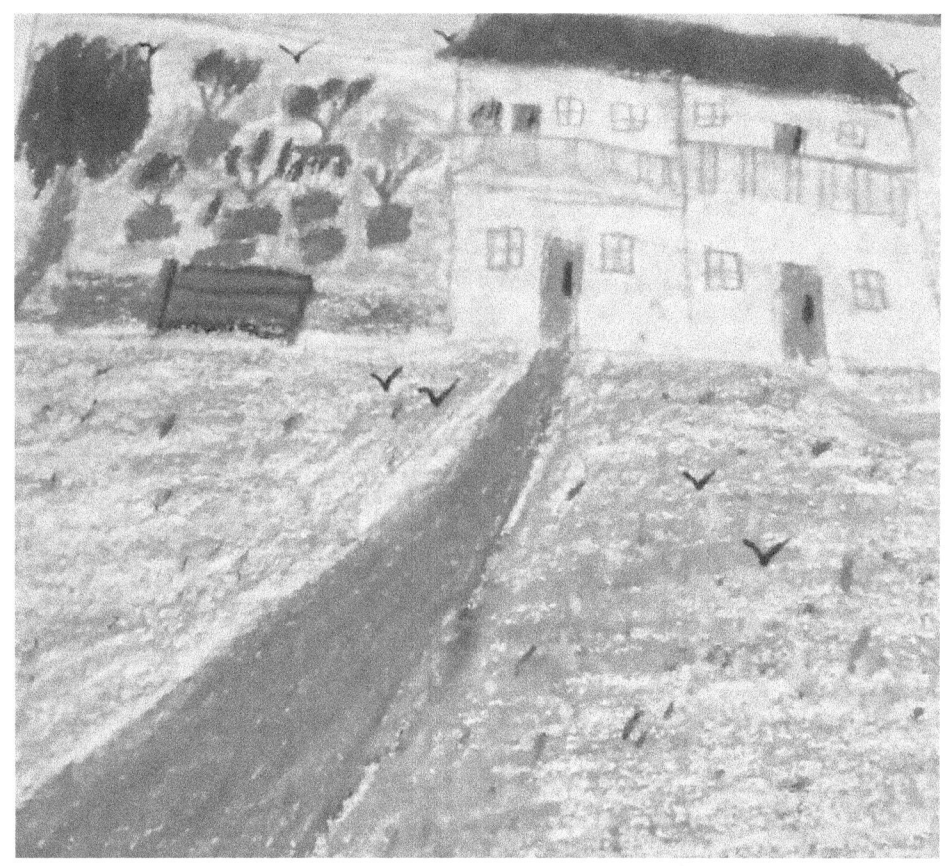

Bliss

(Free Verse)

Their noisy whirring

are no match to your tweeting.

How can people not notice

that your singing gives

such a bliss.

How can they have missed

even your gentle chuckling?

Guide me, fly!

(A poem with no specific rhyming pattern)

Guide me fly,

Soar me high,

In my rhymes I can reach

the stars above,

An angel, you are.

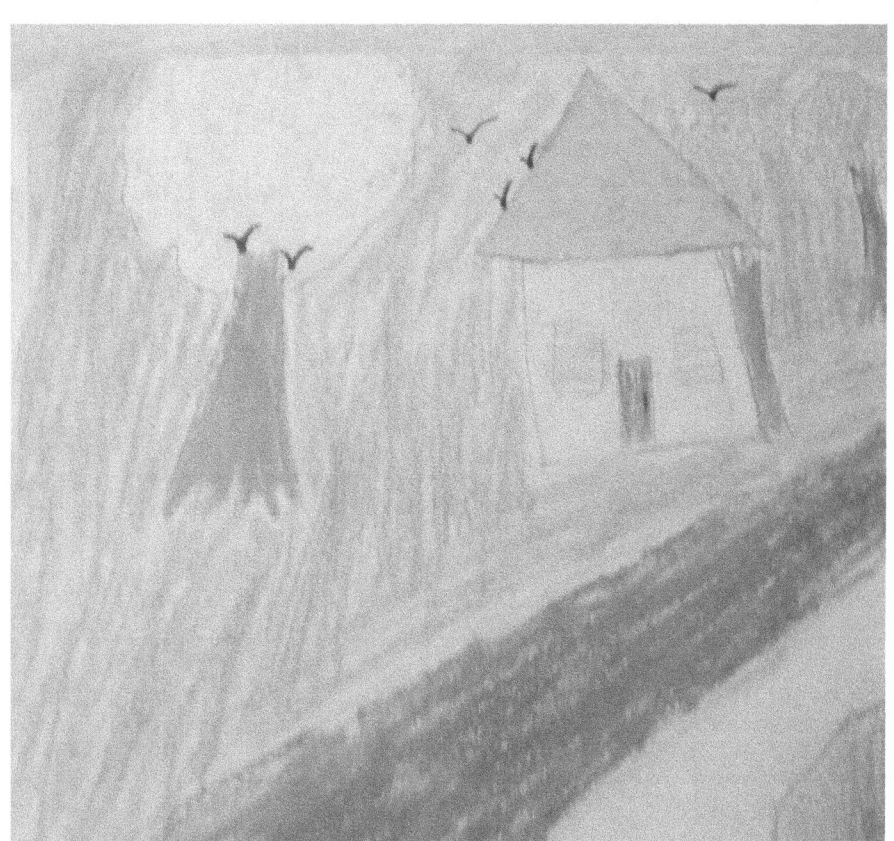

My Angel Bright

(A poem with no specific rhyming pattern)

My angel bright,

looks so right,

' got a happy cooking,

Table is waiting,

but ' am still in my bedroom

looking out for you

on the roofing.

Irony

(Free Verse)

Chaos was there long before,

I lived in peace.

Unkindness, there, was,

I learned to be kind.

I was given to passion,

gentleness, I learned,

and patience.

I cried, I learned to laugh.

I died, I learned to live.

I was in pain, and

evil I saw, I learned to love,

at least in my rhyme.

I want to sing the song of freedom

(An Attempt at a Villanelle)

I want to sing the song of freedom,

I want my children to learn we're born free,

I want them to grow up with wisdom.

I would like to feel that I am loved,

My parents had loved me with all their hearts,

They might have been caught up in the sky above.

I want to sing the song of freedom,

I want to hear my grandchildren laugh,

I want them to grow up in a joyous kingdom.

Walking and running freely is a song of freedom,

Building their bodies and making them tough,

I'd love to see them grow up with wisdom.

Playing hide-and-seek, chasing and running,

   is a song of freedom

Climbing the mountain and looking at the rainbow

   in the end,

I would love to see them grow up with wisdom.

Shining in their games, making their names,

Shaking their booties as they danced in the craze,

I want my grandchildren to sing the song of freedom,

I want them to grow up in wisdom.

EARLIER/OTHER POETRY

A Constant Reminder to Myself

Turn setback into grace,

Sadness into gladness,

Hopelessness to hope,

Repression to freedom,

Depression to liberation of the mind,

Don't allow anyone tell you that you are a disappointment.

Don't allow anyone to manipulate your life.

Keep away from people or materials that want to harm you.

Keep away from people or any material that could possibly hurt or ruin.

Always turn on your smile mechanism.

You are complete and has no need for more.

You are beautiful.

You are pretty

You are good.

Liberated

On quiet days,

interrupted by sonorous little squeaky voices,

your shadow casts a light

on my lethargic state

and I had none a spark.

Your presence brings calm

to my agitated soul.

My hands tied, I struggled to be free.

Thanks to some free souls

I managed to live as I went on in life

With my pen, I am free!

The past is my muse

Shall I leave the past behind?

But the past is me.

They're deep in my consciousness.

To turn your back is ungrateful.

To visit it relieves the soul,

from the tangles and webs of the future.

The past is my muse,

my melody,

the tales I weave in fancy,

the dreams I keep

and fan in my heart,

the treasures I cuddle in my sleep.

Take me by the hand

On a cool, soft meadows,

where the blue sky holds much promise,

and fancies may flow free,

let a bevy of white doves

spread their wings

and cast their embrace

against space and time,

Let the cool breeze give life;

Give life!

Faith

When loneliness creeps in,

and my spirit suffers void,

I need your shadows to guide me.

Desperate we hold on to life,

filling the puzzles that have haunted us,

as we go on with this sphere of journey.

He listens

Worry not,

God will make miracles,

Sooner, later,

It won't be that far,

Hang on with your prayers.

He listens,

Don't give up,

Sooner, later,

He will wipe your tears away,

Hang on with your prayers.

He listens,

It won't be that far.

Reborn

I was only waiting there in sleep

Maybe a thousand years

With only a magic kiss to awaken it

from slumber.

I would rather see it die

and come back to life in its more beautiful form.

Love conquers all

How strange is love

It enhances the emotion

It enhances the mind

It enhances the soul

It captures the beauty of nature

It lives, it breathes,

It conquers time and space

It conquers the world.

My Darling Sweetheart

You made my heart beam with joy
'twas enough to thrill me
To make me laugh
Better yet, feel young once more.

'twas enough to make me strong
To make me do things I can't do
To encourage me to go on living
To live once more.

'twas enough to make me smile at people
To do good to everyone I've come across with
To fill my days and nights.

'twas enough to surmount the difficulties that this life
has to offer
To move heaven and earth
To re-create the beauties of life.

'twas enough to lit the embers of a dying fire
To titillate, to move one's imagination
And re-create a fairy land.

Uninvited Guest

You came as you should come,

uninvited

an unexpected guest in my heart.

You came by the wind,

by the beautiful mountains;

my heart has been filled with joy.

Flood and Sunset

Two hearts wade through flood,

danced in the drizzles.

Their hearts were cheery, no less.

This was passing and it was nothing.

After the downpour came the sunrise.

They enjoyed the soft, gentle hues of the big fire-

ball.

Droopy and teary, but were filled with hope,

for much promise

that tomorrow there would be a bright future.

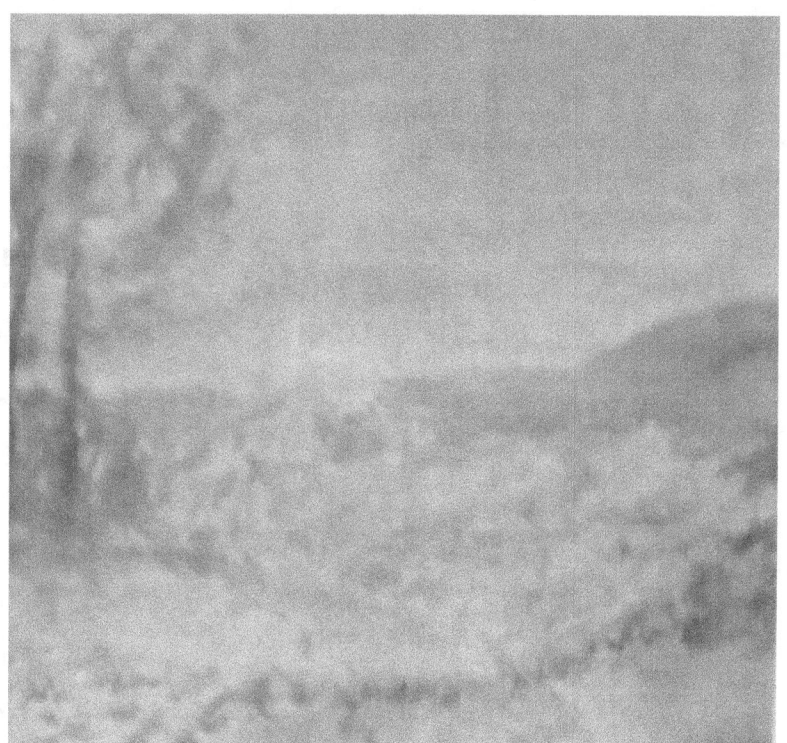

Drift

There is just too much within us

that we have to contend with,

but we can't.

Baffled, all the more, we are,

and lonely.

There are too many scruples around us

that we wanted to live with to avoid dying,

but death stares us in its many forms,

mocking our scruples.

In smiles, in laughters, in tears,

we try to treat ourselves.

We fought, we loosen ourselves, we lost,

then we put the puzzle together.

The brilliant puzzle is about us;

we become whole again.

Love

As long as I have your music
I know I have you inside me.

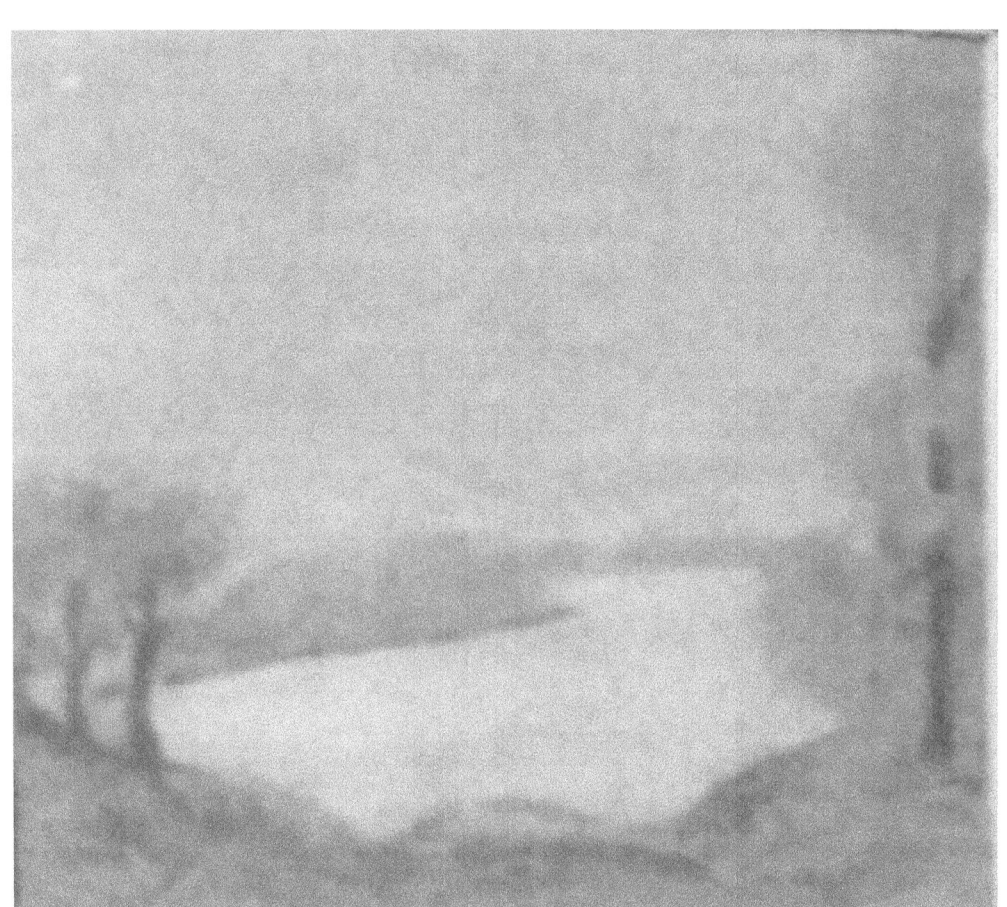

Nostalgia

Tinsels,

Metropolis aglow,

Music floats,

Songs in the air,

Parties,

Puto, bibingka, pansit

Babies in bundles

cooing,

Cats meowing

Dogs barking,

Cool breeze,

Foliages, swaying and dancing,

Voices,

Laughters.

Tree

She moves,

She sways,

gently,

with gracefulness and ease,

Then she kissed and hugged,

Her body full of life,

Full of love,

She rises,

Looked up in supplication?

or praise?

Then she went back to her dance.

Love

Love breathes through loneliness,

In the middle of the noise and the haste

it is a singular voice,

It's a powerful image among throngs of bodies,

It's a pulse that beats faster by the distance,

A stream that ceaselessly flows.

It is your compass,

It is your guide,

It is your music,

It is your truth,

It is your inspiration—and desperation, oh, yes!

It is your scourge—and your healing,

It is your death—and rebirth.

Jason

There is never a thing this boy can't hurdle.

A matchbox can be a car;

the stick, a sword.

A few penny can be aplenty.

A little spark, a star.

A boat can be a ship,

a pain, a glory,

an injury, happiness,

a stream of water, sea,

a sea, an ocean, a journey.

There is never a thing this boy can't handle.

Heaven-sent

See those eyes that barely speak,

Bugs you when you're wrong,

Lighten up your heart, too?

Makes you smile,

Makes you sad,

Makes you excited, thrilled?

Crazy... the joy of loving?

Complicated? Or you need a wide range of
emotions?

But emotions drift...

In a moment you are ecstatic,

Another moment you are mad,

Another moment you're much in love,

At another moment you are angry,

Do you want to scream? Say dumbass!

Crazy... that head of yours?

Passions explode

But as you look at those eyes

you feel guilty, somehow,

It was your expectations,

But commitment is another... not all pass the test of
time.

Eg's Poem

In paradise is where I live,

Where the beauty of nature meets,

A little trickle of rain,

A little sun,

Moon, sun, and rainbows abound,

Where the angels frolic among birds and plants,

And when the sunset comes, I heave a sigh,

What heaven, what wonder, what peace.

Ode To Friendship

Can we pause a while?

Take a break?

Let's have a little chat.

It does not take much to strike a conversation.

I have coffee to offer,

while you have cookies and chocolates.

Let us pause a while,

Take a break.

You can be yourself with your antics,

or we can talk about the latest news, and kitchen

views.

Let us pause a while,

Take a break.

How fast time flies!

In intrigues, and in controversies

you stood your ground, I stood mine.

But shall these stop us from being friends?

235

Can we pause a while?

Take a break?

Look at ourselves.

It doesn't take much to be heroic.

All it takes is a little smile.

Repugnant Angel

I am awed, I basked at the beauty of two souls loving
I am amazed how they bend to charm,
　　to kindness, to romancing, to guttural sounds,
　　like birds exchanging, pecking beak to beak,
Twitting, greeting, chirruping until the sounds
　　rapturously explode, like singing, bringing heaven
　　on *terra firma*.

She has fallen asleep under my arms, feeling secure,
She feels she's under the wings of an angel, who looks
　　over her like a lover.
She sleeps like a baby, putting all the pillows around
　　her,
She doesn't mind her surroundings because she feels
　　safe with me;
 She doesn't know I'm her lover.

A World Without Horizon

I live by the mountains,

By the cool winds,

Fresh morning dews,

Birds that sing,

Trees that gracefully dance,

By the glorious fields,

By the radiant sun,

Splendid dawn

and of bountiful harvest,

By the gentle streams and springs,

By the brilliant stars and moon that cradles my

dream,

By poems and stories that feed the heart,

By poets and poetesses whose language is love.

I live by a world with no horizon

Where days are young

Where rains or storms

and summers

are all my friends.

Cigarette

The solid fire burns,

An earthen mold,

Smooth, on the surface I am drawn,

Made hard to be sturdy,

Made soft to be resilient to any touch,

Deep thoughts,

Overwhelming passions,

Anger, depression,

Joys and pains,

It was made to be there,

Try as it may

can't assume a distinct personality,

It was made for the user,

The user, its master,

It was there to absorb emotion,

Life hangs on, precariously,

Puff ... bellow,

One, two... ten,

Clock ticked fast,

It's over.

Jimbo

Can't find any of you today

Went on with my walking

Was looking around for your craze

But there wasn't any of your trace.

Dup, dup, bup, bup

Dum, dum, boom, boom

Set my mood upbeat

I have to beat the heat within me.

I can't be beaten

My mood swings can be driven.

Get on.

Move on.

I want to go back to the past

I want to go back to the past

when life was simple yet sweet,

When I would strum my guitar

and fill the wind with my song,

When friends would sit for a game or tale,

When I'd be lost in the field

and walk on the soft meadows,

Dance with the birds, trees, and the bees,

When I could climb the mountain

and fill my parched throat with spring water,

When the sun and sky were clear

and the air was clean,

I want to go back to the past,

when nature's beauty was unspoiled.

A Child's World

Let a child grow in an atmosphere of freedom,

He makes his future.

But, hush … not too much … to make his head too

strong,

A gentle word of caution will temper his pride.

Let a child grow in an atmosphere of equality,

He will defend it to the end when he gets older.

But, hush… remind him not to be a bigot,

Because they may have their points, too.

Let a child grow in an atmosphere of love,

He will make life throughout life.

I will kiss the earth

I will kiss the earth,

its nocturnal beauty,

its quiet peace.

I will let its cool embrace

touch my cheek, my face,

and feel its solemn passion.

I will seize the day

with faith,

I will seize its glory.

I will kiss the earth,

Let it touch me,

I will seek refuge under the wide leaves

of its trees.

The branches are my strength,

Then, I'll dance,

I will kiss the earth.

Breath

You are the spirit that guides my way,

The joy behind my smile,

The breeze that fans my heart,

The little tickles of my fancies,

I daydream, feeling you are around,

Your laughter chases me,

Your sadness disturbs me,

Your eccentricities annoy me, but charm me no less,

Your stubbornness I hated,

But your idiocies I came to love,

Your mediocrities are part of my nostalgia,

You are the reason why I have become patient,

and sentient, and still.

You are the force that makes me go on with this

journey,

The wind beneath my wings,

You are what pushes my pen to write,

The reason I see things in its own light,

wish brilliance upon a circumstance,

-and enlightenment upon your soul,

That you may see and feel what is right,

And I wish upon a star,

And I wish things will be alright,

Inspite of all the sufferings,

Or how can I afford to laugh, and laugh still?

You are perfect!

Your love is free as a dove in the sky,

As warm as the shine of the morning sun,

Quiet and serene as waters of spring,

I got up thinking what we've been all through.

You were perfect though imperfect,

You don't complain as I do complain,

I can be on top of my voice but you're a calm water,

You let the ride by

as if the roads are straight,

My wit is dying but your humor has no end.

Something has come about.

Nothing can kill your will,

We have the right to exist in this world,

and be happy,

and live peacefully on our own,

You went by your daily job with or without clients,

Endlessly you wrote to make both ends meet.

You are the peace, the calm,

You bore the difficulties without protest,

You are patience,

You are perseverance,

You are strength.

Nothing distracts you,

Haven't heard you laugh aloud,

Nor swear, nor badmouth me,

Nor touch me,

You worked with quiet joy for someone you love,

Nothing is an impediment,

You are an astute mind,

I can hear the tweeting birds;

I know I am loved.

Apology of an Introvert

Forgive me, I do not intend to be rude
   it's my mood,
My head cranks, I wanted to open the door
   but then I brood,
I might not give you the face that you want,
   that'd be ingratitude,
Allow me to sleep it off, or I'll lie in my bed,
   til I get my groove.

Am not a party-goer, but that doesn't mean
   I dislike you,
I may not like you on social media, but that doesn't
   mean I disapprove of you,
In fact, I find liking ALL that's posted on social media
   abhorrent, not of you, but of the attitude,
Aren't we made to use our mind,
   isn't that more cool, dude?

Don't give me anything, then ask me to LIKE you,

I am forever grateful, that's in my heart, for sure,

Don't push the algorithm, it's fine, it's made to be there,

Your images I've always liked because I don't have
much of social life.

If I don't click the LIKE button, it's alright,

God has made us not to be always right,

But don't tell me to friend or old friends because they
may not like,

It may boomerang to me or to you and our blood may
spike.

We have good memories, that should be enough,

There's no more spoiling our days, we'll be all right,

We all have problems on our own, I don't have
            to announce to ALL.

But God has assured us, we'll be fine, we'll be well.

My fingers are numbing and my head is light,

It means too much exposure to radiation is not right,

So don't push your beautiful or handsome face on me,

Or make me believe everything I see.

If it doesn't make sense, I LEAVE the page,

If it pushes the crap out of me, I DEACTIVATE.

A Child's Prayer

Free Verse

I'm a child of God,

Contrite,

Obedient to His Will,

I do the best I can,

Leave to God the rest.

There's a blessing of inner peace,

   and of quiet joy

    accomplished through prayer.

The truth lies in Him

   to whom we owe our creation.

My sadness turns into gladness,

My pain to resilience,

My uncertainty to faith

To God in whom I trust.

Peace to all and the blessings of life

is my daily greeting,

Good morning and good day,

None that can spoil my mood,

God allow me to sustain my groove

    throughout the day,

So that at night I can say my evening prayer,

Thank God and have a restful sleep.

Pleasures of the Heart

The flowers blooming and swaying with the gentle breeze,

The verdant plants and trees catching up with the soul's commune,

The quiet voices of angels, the brushes of broomsticks are simple bliss,

Small trumpets and kitty's antics complete such heaps of joy.

What an ardent heart's desire can not accomplish when it wish,

The sun lit up in the east prepared to wield its friendly stroke,

The tiny footsteps and cherubs beaming, my heart catches up peace,

Then I heard you enter the door with a basket-full, oh! boy.

What can not appease a heart hard to please?

To humble hearts I bow, theirs are pure solid gold.

Becoming Old

Even the slightest movement of your leg is a hurdle,

You take care of the gauze on the left,

And you take care your right won't get wet,

It is at this stage that a person has learned grace—

at his or her own pace,

Graceful as you sit,

Graceful as you walk,

Graceful as you move your fingers,

Graceful as you talk,

Graceful as you smile at people

who have come later in your life,

and you never knew you would meet.

It is at this stage that generosity visits you... and kindness.

A Stream of Consciousness from Psalms

You filled my cup, my half-empty cup.

My heart was lonely, but you made me smile;
  you wiped away my tears.
I had no energy, yet you kept me moving and going.
There was no laughter in my lips but my delight came
    right on time; my heart was pleased,
    and so much more, and even more.
I was filled with anxiety but you assured me that things
    would be alright.
I was filled with so many mundane worries, but you
    taught me to manage my daily life.
I had no real friends, but you kept me company.
I've been shaken for years, but you kept me standing,
   and steady.
You said I was stronger than I thought,
that my real power is inside me,

Convincing me that God alone is enough.

The smallest things
are the sweetest
and the most endearing.

Where is truth, but in our hearts,

as old as the universe,

as brilliant as the sun.

ABOUT THE AUTHOR

Anadelfa Samson-Bernardo was a former public servant and a teacher. Her works, The Banquet Hall series, Magical Birds, A Piece of Heaven, Born to be Princess, Puset and the Hunt for the Magic Mirror, A Short Interlude, The Swimming Party, The Anxious Kitten and other Short Stories, and Diwata are published online by Amazon, Barnes and Nobles, m.webnovel.com, Scifier.com, thriftbooks.com, bookshop.org, takealot.com, and dymocks.com.au, to name a few platforms.

Bibliography

Shakespeare; Sonnet 50

https://citeseerx.ist.psu.edu/document?repid=rep1&type=pdf&doi
=e7f2b5b789f68f307b4436e2e073c3baea89e016

Shakespeare; Sonnet 50

https://en.wikipedia.org/wiki/Sonnet_50

Pope's metrical rhyme

https://www.jstor.org/stable/27703073

Petrarchan rhyme

https://interestingliterature.com/2023/05/best-examples-of-
petrarchan-sonnets/#

Alighieri, Dante; metrical style

https://poets.org/glossary/terza-rima

Homer's Iliad

https://classics.mit.edu/Homer/iliad.1.i.html